A Parents' Guide To

Preparing for Independent School Interviews

Dedicated to my parents for their sacrifice, my husband for his friendship and love, my children for their laughter and above all, God who allows for horizons to exist.

Table of Contents

Chapter 1

What Happens in an Interview?

Most children will not have had an interview before. They are either quite laid back, not realising the gravity of the situation, or terrified of what's to come. Most will lie in between.

Every interview will have a one-to-one element. Interviewers want to get to know your child. They want to form an overall impression or look for that certain spark, which can only be done with a face to face assessment.

Most will have one interviewer, but some schools can have two, up to three – someone with special needs training for example may sit on the panel (Westminster School). Certain schools like to have a group interview (Highgate) *in addition* to the one-to-one, which may involve a practical element.

Typical interviews last 30 minutes and are conducted on school grounds. Much to the delight of the child, parents are also 'interviewed' at some establishments (Haberdashers' School).

According to Kings' Recruitment 38% of employers did not hire the candidate because of voice quality, overall confidence level and a lack of smile.

Chapter 2

Does My Child Need to Practice?

As with advice about the written exams the official line is 'no' but practical answer is 'yes'. When you ask your child for the first time to talk about their hobbies and interests, no matter how articulate, they will stumble. Suddenly their mind goes blank and they can't think of all the extra-curricular things you have been ferrying them to for the last 8 years!

Children have a lot to say, the information is floating around in their brain. Practising questions **organises** that information in a logical way, so they can present it. It is NOT about rehearsing answers. It is about providing them with tools to have the confidence and ease to talk about themselves. Which by nature, is not a task that comes easily.

Certain questions will come up in every interview, while other questions you cannot prepare for. Nonetheless by teaching your child reasoning and logical skills, providing them with an orderly way to present their thoughts, it will do wonders.

Children are more likely to adhere to techniques that are simple and short. The strategies in this book are those that I have found most effective in my daily practice.

Chapter 3

What Are Schools Looking For?

They are looking for those who are **"able"**

- **PERSON ABLE**

  What is your child like beyond the classroom; their hobbies and interests.

- **TEACH ABLE**

  Willing to learn, and if necessary be willing to unlearn and relearn.

- **CHALLENGE ABLE**

  Discuss topical issues; see other viewpoints and critically analyse them.

- **CONSCIOUS ABLE**

  What are their thoughts on moral issues: euthanasia, climate control, animal testing etc.

- **KNOWLEDGE ABLE**

  They may be given some English and Maths questions; they want to understand *how* your child arrived at their answer.

- **SUPPORT ABLE**

  How does your child interact with their peers, are they a team player?

- **COMFORT ABLE**

  Will they fit into this school?

Chapter 4

Preparation for the Interview

As well as going through some questions in advance, there are many things your child can do to help prepare for the interview.

1. Keep abreast of current affairs and political issues

Be aware of the important issues facing the world. In this digital-age we know in an instant about affairs across the globe. Information is at our fingertips, so ignorance is not a valid excuse.

Children should develop social awareness. The root word of 'politics' is from the Greek *Politiko* which means affairs of the cities. Being politically aware means having your say on legislation from tax, health care, the environment, to schooling. Matters which affect us all. It is therefore a skill for life.

In essence, as parents we are constantly engaged in politics within our own small 'cities' i.e. families. A view supported by our former Prime Minister Margaret Thatcher, *"you know, there is no such thing as society. There are individual men and women and there are families."*

As parents, we should foster and nurture a child's interest in politics; all the while creating an awareness that we should respect other viewpoints that do not agree with our own. American Professor Leo Buscaglia sums it up perfectly *"I have a very strong feeling that the opposite of love is not hate - it's apathy. It's not giving a damn."*

Here are my top tips:

READ THE NEWS DAILY.

> Whatever format it may be: magazines, websites, news alerts on your phone, just make sure your child knows what's going on in the world.

DISCUSS ISSUES AROUND THE DINNER TABLE

Learn to listen to other view points and argue against them (in a polite manner!). Can your child see *why* the other person has that opinion? How did mummy or daddy come to that conclusion?

TRY ROLE PLAY.

Ask your child if they were a politician what would be the most important issue they would want to change? Can they think of how they would go about it?

OFFER AN ALTERNATIVE VIEWPOINT.

When reading an article, do not try to force your child to agree with the journalist's point of view. What do **they** think of Mr. Trump?

2. Keep the Hobbies and Interests Going

A common mistake, parents feel the need to stop all extra-curricular activities. Not only do these help your child into being that well-rounded person (which is what schools are looking for), it is an outlet for stress, a source of friendship and a skill they can continue in life.

When writing their UCAS forms for universities, personal statements are just for this kind of thing. All-work-no-play is not an environment that will foster learning.

Keep a portfolio and written record of their achievements and hobbies. For the interview, you may want to do a mind map so they can have their information at their fingertips

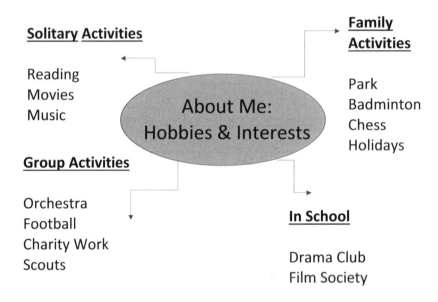

Solitary Activities

Reading
Movies
Music

Group Activities

Orchestra
Football
Charity Work
Scouts

About Me: Hobbies & Interests

Family Activities

Park
Badminton
Chess
Holidays

In School

Drama Club
Film Society

As you can see, we are just **organising** not rehearsing answers. Despite what others may say, preparation is KEY. They should be able to elaborate a few sentences on each hobby: *what they like, any challenges they overcame, what they have got out of it (even if just friendship).*

Be prepared to talk about 2 or 3 books they have read, know a little about the authors. *Why did they like that book, how would they change it, what is their favourite character* and so on. It is important to choose a book they like, not force them to select a Charles Dickens novel!

3.Open Days

Like a job interview you research the company you are applying for, so go and see the school. Note what you like and did not like. This will help answer those **'why do you want to come here'** questions. Read the prospectus and have a look at the list of clubs on offer. This will also help formulate an answer when asked **'do you have any questions for us?'**

4. Practice!

In the next chapter are a list of common questions that have been used. Get a neighbour or a friend to practise on your child. If they say 'I read the news and was sad to see the amazon fires,' press them further. *Why were you sad? What is the effect of that in the world? Why do you think this is an important issue? What can you do to help?*

Did you know that 65% of the population are visual learners, mind maps are a great way to learn.

Chapter 5

50 Interview Questions to Practice with Your Child

About You

1. Tell me about your family. Do you have brothers or sisters?

2. What activities do you do as a family? How was your weekend?

3. Tell me about your hobbies and interests.

4. What did you do over the summer holidays?

5. Do you like watching TV? What programmes do you like?

6. What book are you reading? Tell me about it.

7. What is your favourite book? How would you change the ending?

8. What is your favourite character in a book or film?

9. Do you like to play sports? Are you in a team or a club?

10. Do you play an instrument? What do you like about it?

11. Do you sing, do you go to concerts?

12. Tell me about your favourite holiday destination.

13. What are your three best qualities?

14. What are your two worst qualities?

15. What do you want to be when you are older?

16. Are you involved in any charity work?

17. How would your best friend describe you?

18. Do you go to the theatre or plays?

19. What's better a book or a play/film?

Your school

20. Do you like your current school? What do you like most about it?

21. What is your favourite subject?

22. What is your least favourite subject?

23. What is your greatest achievement at your school?

24. How do you see yourself in forty years?

25. Tell me about a time you worked as a team?

26. What after-school activities do you do?

27. Do you have any school responsibilities like prefect, monitor? What have you learnt from those roles?

28. Is there anything you will change about your school?

29. Tell me about a difficult time in school and how you overcame it.

30. You are on the school football team (or netball, choir, adapt appropriately) and one of your peers are not performing well, how could you motivate them?

School you are applying to

31. What about this school appeals to you?

32. What did you like on the open day?

33. Is there anything about this school that you think would be challenging for you?

34. What would you look forward to doing if you came here?

35. Why do you think this school will suit you?

36. Are you applying to other schools?

Challenging questions

37. If you could go back in history, which time would you go back to and why?

38. Who is your hero? Who inspires you?

39. If you were given 200 pounds, what would you do with it?

40. Think of as many things as possible that you could do with this tie.

41. Is winning always important?

News or Topical Issues

42. Can you tell me anything significant that is happening now; globally or locally?

43. Open a newspaper/magazine and ask their thoughts on any topical issues e.g. Brexit – should there be a referendum? What are your thoughts of Boris Johnson being Prime minister of UK when the public did not vote for him?

44. What do you think about social media?

45. Is gaming addictive?

46. What do you think of private education?

47. What do you think of single sex education?

48. Should school aged children be allowed to vote?

Final questions

49. Is there anything about yourself that you haven't told us?

50. Do you have any questions for me?

These interview questions are also traditionally used by employers. Going through this exercise will provide you with tools throughout your adult life!

Chapter 6

The 5 Most Common Pitfalls

1. ONE-WORD ANSWERS

Interviewer: *Do you play an instrument?*

Student: *Yes*

A preferred technique is to employ full and developed sentences.

Student: *Yes I play guitar I am grade 5, I find playing music helps relax me. My favourite pieces of music are... I played in the concert also.*

2. OVER-REHEARSED ANSWERS

Interviewer: *Do you have siblings?*

Student 1:   *Yes I have siblings we fight a lot but I use my negotiation skills I learnt on the communication skills course to help overcome the situation.*

Student 2:	*No we never fight we always get on, we have a perfect family.*

These ring alarm bells that the student has been prepped – interviewers do not like this at all. Both answers seem far from the truth. Avoid at all costs, keep the interviewer happy.

3. LOOKING BORED

Body language is key. I will talk about this in the later section. Having a child whose yawning, having minimal eye contact, not smiling, bored or fidgety is off-putting for the Interviewer. Can you imagine, why would the school want to teach someone like this? It would be a chore for them. They are looking for 'teach-ability' and someone who is personable; can get on well with others, while being respectful.

4. STATING THE SCHOOL IS NOT THEIR FIRST CHOICE

An obvious point but you would be surprised how many children state this. Or they may say their parents want them to go to this school. Schools have hundreds of applicants, why not choose someone who wants to be there? A big no-no.

5. NOT DOING THE RESEARCH

One child in their interview said they could not wait to use the hockey pitch when in fact the school did not have a hockey pitch. Know the school, do your research. These things leave a bad taste and can easily be avoided.

A 2014 survey by New CareerBuilder concluded that almost ¾ of employers say they look for a 'positive attitude' in candidates

Chapter 7

Non-Verbal Cues: What to do with Those Fidgety Hands!

It takes 5-30 seconds to form a first impression. Visual cues are a big part of that. Follow these practical tips:

- *Wear something smart*

  School uniform is a good option, especially if your child attends one of the feeder schools. So, we need: polished shoes, cleaned and iron clothes, shirts tucked in and buttons all closed. Tie and a blazer for boys (not a blazer that is too small or too big).

- *Be on time*

  This means parents, you need to find out where you are going to park! Check google maps for traffic incidents. Do a dummy run. Children who are late are often flustered; it disorganizes their thought process. Your body language will reflect your state of mind. A relaxed, calm and confident demeanour is what we are aiming for.

- *Right mind-set*

  Be positive, give a firm handshake when your child arrives. Schools want someone they are not going to have to work on much i.e. an already packaged pupil. Ask them to smile, to show your child is friendly and will fit in at this school.

- *Walk with an air of confidence*

  As your child is being led to the interview room suggest they look ahead, some light banter with the interviewer is always a bonus!

- *Sit up straight*

  Slightly forward as it shows they are listening and engaged with the interviewer.

- *Maintain eye contact*

  This shows they are not afraid and paying attention.

- *In the waiting room*

  Try not to play with your phone or let your child play with theirs; take a book or magazine, it forms a good impression. Have the mind-frame that your child is on display as soon as they enter the building.

- *Hands*

  Encourage your child to keep their hands uncrossed and discourage them to touch their face. It is a sign they may be nervous, also when people lie they touch their nose and ears. It is best to keep them on their lap. Crossed arms can signify a defensive position.

- *If they get nervous*

  Tell them to push their hands into their lap or push their feet into the ground; the interviewer cannot tell they are worried and it will dissipate that nervous energy.

- *Stop those swinging legs*

  Some children swing their legs when nervous. Have them sit slightly forwards and feet firmly on the ground.

It's NOT crazy to talk to yourself. Positive affirmations can help motivate your child. Stick them on the bathroom mirror to look at when brushing teeth.

Chapter 8

A Word About Group Interviews

Unlike the panel or one-to-one interviews, it is not so easy to prepare. However, for the interviewer(s) it gives them an opportunity to see how they interact with their peers, stand out from the crowd, solve problems and see whether they are a team player.

Questions can be in the form of:

- Problem solving - working with others to solve a problem and come up with an answer.

- Group Task – could be a physical activity.

- Group Presentation

- Discussing a moral or controversial issue such as euthanasia.

Skills needed for a group interview

- *Be prepared* to talk about themselves and explain why they want to come to this school.

- *Be confident* through their body language and speech (not too quiet or too loud).

- *Listen* and show others they are interested in what they are saying.

Do

Say something memorable about yourself e.g. you play the bazooka

Show you're a team player and support what others are saying and be willing to change your own viewpoint

Come across as likeable – smile and nod

Be polite don't shout or interrupt, respect viewpoints that do not agree with your own

---

Don't

Stay quiet throughout, answering once in a while in a soft voice

Come across as arrogant and avoid defensive postures such as sitting with their arms crossed

Leader

Listener

Group Interviews

Keep The Balance

Chapter 9

Thinking Outside the Box

These are the questions children dread but often will identify the Scholarship candidates. **There is no right or wrong here, they are testing the thought process**. Encourage your child to think about the systems they used in their writing:

- The 5 senses

- The 5 W's: Who What, Why, Where, When

- For Vs Against

Any system is fine to use as long as they have a system, justify their answer and they have thought beyond the obvious.

Interviewer:	*Tell me about this object*
Student 1:	*It's an orange you eat it*

Using the "senses' approach

Student 2:	*This orange is a food item, people may eat it as part of a healthy diet (taste), it has nice aroma so you may use it in cooking (smell), oranges can be used as decoration on a bowl (sight).*

Chapter 10

Final Words of Advice

A child who is confident will do better in an interview than one who is not. **Preparation** is what gives confidence. It will stop a child fumbling around for answers with *'err'* and *'umm'*.

No doubt children will face an interview process again in their life, so the experience will put them in good stead.

The night before the interview:

- GET A GOOD NIGHT'S SLEEP

Stay focused, do not try to learn any new information.

- A GOOD DIET

Sugar/caffeine/junk food can make us feel sluggish or skittish so avoid these. Help them stay hydrated to help concentration. Ideal foods include bananas which have natural sugars to give that boost of energy and omega 3 foods (such as chia seeds) which provide protein for the brain.

- GO FOR A BRISK WALK

Exercise gets oxygen to the brain and releases happy hormones, it facilitates the growth of new brain cells. We know children who exercise, sleep better.

- VISUALIZE

Many top athletes use visualization before an important game. Change into their smart clothes and do a mental rehearsal of the interview. Tell your child to visualise it going well, use all their senses and create a vivid picture in their mind.

Unless specified in the interview letter there is no need to take anything with you to the interview. However, for any badges your

child has earned such as 'monitor' or 'captain,' have your child wear them with pride and be prepared to talk about them.

Scientists at New Mexico State University showed that basketball players who visualised free throw success before a game had an increase in real success in the actual game

---

Finally…

REFLECT.

If your child has another interview impending analyse their previous one:

- what went well - repeat those

- what didn't go well - how could you change this?

Remember there are no failures. Each experience is a lesson in life, it is all about growth. Reward them for their efforts.

While every effort has been made to make sure the information in this guide is accurate, please check with each school regarding the interview format. Interview arrangements are also subject to change.

About the Author

As a medical doctor who specialises in Child Health, Afrosa has worked with young people over many years. This has been in her capacity as a General Practitioner, School Governor, GP Tutor to medical students and a mother; guiding her own children through the process, ultimately being awarded scholarships.

She sits on the interview panel for two leading London Russell Group Universities. Consequently, she has been awarded unique interview training from these establishments.

From her own consultations and training with children, she shares her practical tips to overcome nerves and stress.

"After preparation for the written papers, children and parents often loose steam. With this book, I provide a simple step-by-step guide so you can navigate your child with ease.

Over time I have conducted many mock interviews and the feedback from clients has always been over-whelming. I hope I have facilitated in making the final leg of this journey less arduous.

Good luck!"

DR AFROSA AHMED

To arrange a mock interview please email
11plusinterviews@gmail.com

These sessions can be conducted in person or online.
More tips and advice on the Facebook page:
https://www.facebook.com/11plusinterviews/

Printed in Great Britain
by Amazon

36539822R00022